I Will Always Remember You

Written and Illustrated
by Jessica Hooks

I Will Always Remember You

A heartwarming story about a daughter remembering the good times she had with her father. This is an uplifting story that will remind you that every memory is a precious gift.

I remember as far back when I was a baby. Something as simple as you holding me made me feel so safe. The warmth of your chest, the strong beat of your heart and the loving support of your arms. I will always remember you.

I remember seeing you walk and me saying, "Down, down daddy, I walk too." Right then and there I knew I could walk just like you. I will always remember you.

I remember the wrestling matches. Hulk Hogan and Andre the Giant on our little t.v and me jumping on your back trying to take you down. You patting the floor while counting "1,2,3." I will always, remember you.

I remember the first story you read to me, Green Eggs and Ham. Me saying "Oh daddy can we have some too." You smiling and saying, "Yea, but make my eggs blue." I will always remember you.

I remember music coming from your room. Me walking in and seeing you and mom dancing to your favorite tunes. That was a good day. That was a special moment. I will always remember you.

I remember you walking me to the bus stop. I was running late that day. Me looking back while shouting and running, "Bye daddy I love you!" And you yelling back, "I love you more, please learn something today." I will always remember you.

I remember my first bike ride. Me falling down one time or maybe two. You, telling me, "Daddy got you, keep going, you'll never fall as long as I'm with you." I will always remember you.

I remember when we had career day at school. I was so proud of you. You showed my class why I thought my daddy was so cool. I will always remember you.

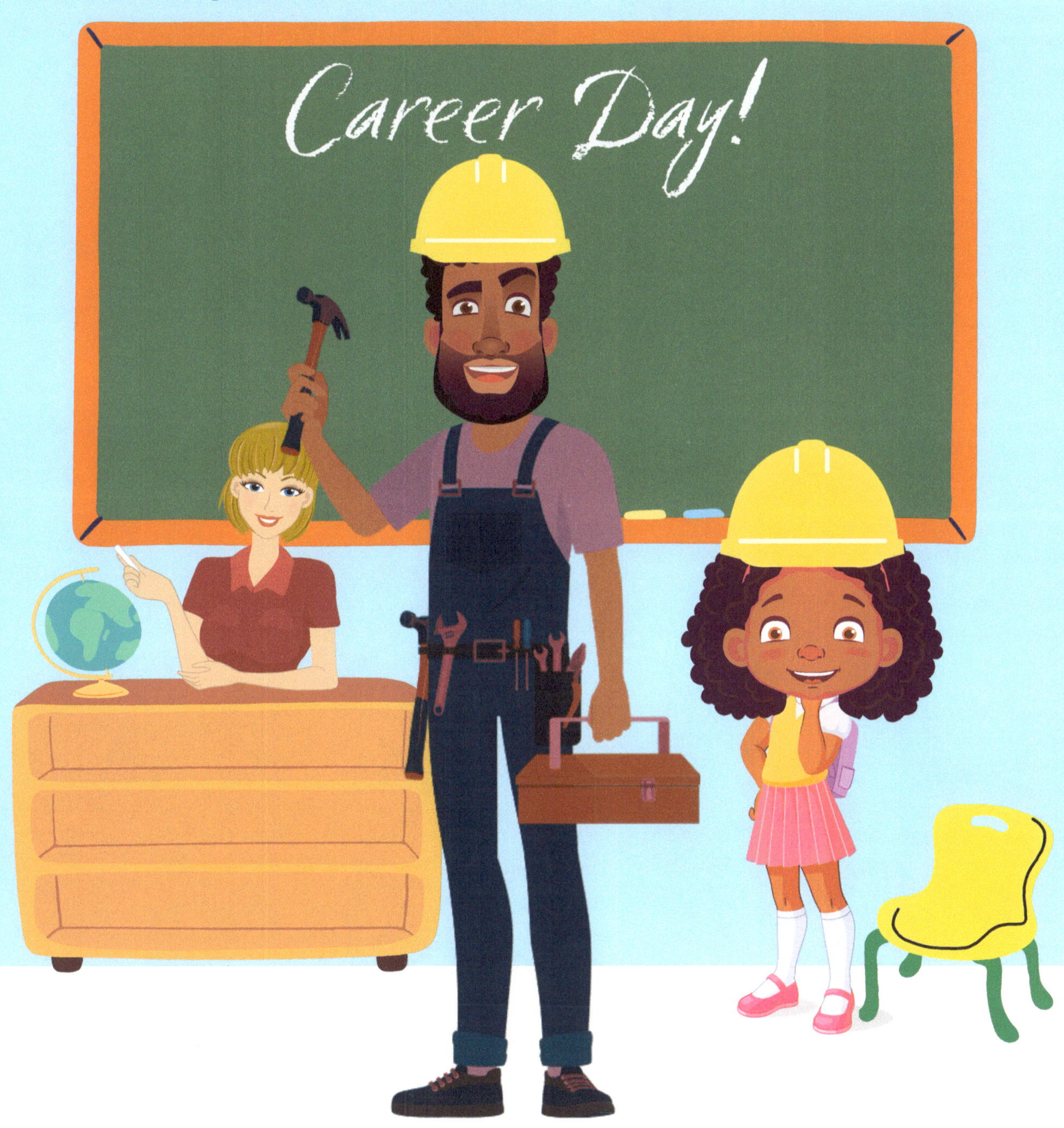

I remember being really nervous for my big dance recital. You helping me get over my nervousness while making silly jokes pretending to be a one-eyed pirate. I will always remember you.

I remember when I told you I wanted to be a skateboarder. You told me you wanted to be one too. You tried so hard to keep your balance, but that didn't go so well for you. I will always remember you.

I remember coming home from school and smelling the food that you prepared. You were so proud to display your meal. You would say, "Get prepared to taste the best meal around. My famous grilled steak, seasoned so good you'll lick the plate!" I will always remember you.

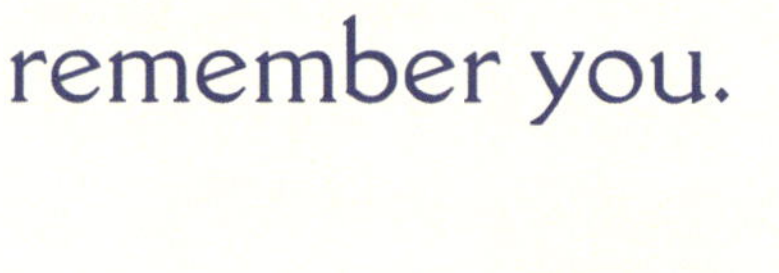

Though years have passed, and you're gone now. Every memory of you will continue to live on. My heart will forever remain full of joy because, I will always remember you.

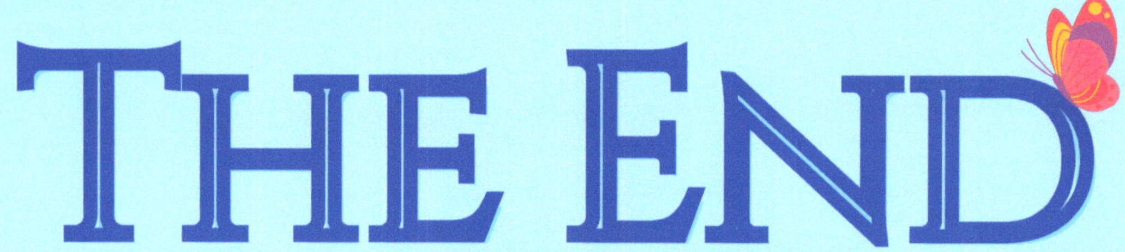
THE END

Dedicated to my Daddy,
Stanley Earl Felder.
I will always remember you!

If You like this book, Check out these books.

Don't forget about these!

Little Black Girl You Are:

A book about a little girl loving herself throughout the challenges placed in front of her. Watch this little girl discover just how her bravery can inspire and uplift others. This book will teach children how to build self-confidence while celebrating their unique gifts.

By the end of the book children will learn self-worth, confidence, and diversity. Little Black Girl You Are, will inspire and uplift kids while showing them the real magic is within them!

PAW-PAW TEACHES US ABOUT BLACK INVENTORS

Join Sasha and Timothy as they learn how African American inventors changed the world. In this book Sasha and Timothy visits their Pawpaw (Grandpa), who reads to them a book about Black Inventors. He teaches them how black inventors had a hand in everything we still use today. This book will not only inform kids about the great minds behind important inventions, but it will also show them how a single idea can change the world forever.

Will Bud make Good choices or Bad choices?

What will Bud do when his mom lets him make his own choices? Will he make Good choices or Bad choices? Help Bud as he decides which path to choose.

Phillip's Birthday Suprise

It's Phillip's birthday, and he's sure his friends will celebrate his special day with him. There's just one problem...no one seems to remember his birthday. Have Phillip's friends forgotten all about his big day?

Two Homes Twice The Love

Alexis and Jonathan's parents have remarried, but it doesn't stop their parents from showing them just how much they love them. Join Alexis and Jonathan as they give you a glimpse into their lives to show you how having two homes equal twice the love.

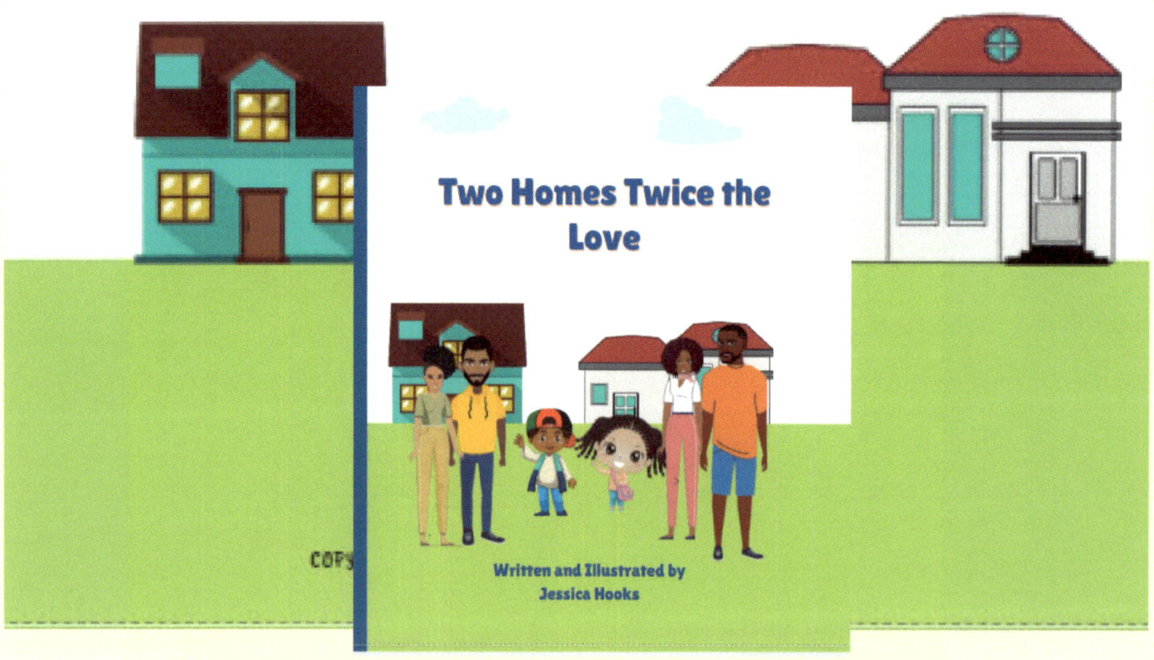